MW00668591

12 Christmas Favorites

High Voice

Edited by Richard Walters

Caroling, Caroling • The Christmas Song • Do You Hear What I Hear •
Gesù Bambino • Go, Tell It on the Mountain • I Heard the Bells on Christmas Day •
I Wonder as I Wander • I'll Be Home for Christmas • O Holy Night • Silver Bells •
Some Children See Him • White Christmas

ISBN-13: 978-0-634-08182-8
ISBN-10: 0-634-08182-9

HAL•LEONARD® CORPORATION
7777 W. BLUEMOUND RD. P.O. BOX 13819 MILWAUKEE, WI 53213

Visit Hal Leonard Online at
www.halleonard.com

Contents

Page		Full Performance	Piano Accompaniments
4	Caroling, Caroling*	1	13
9	The Christmas Song**	3	15
6	Do You Hear What I Hear**	2	14
12	Gesù Bambino (with violin or cello)*	4	16
19	violin part		
20	cello part		
26	Go, Tell It on the Mountain*	6	18
23	I Heard the Bells on Christmas Day*	5	17
30	I Wonder as I Wander*	7	19
34	I'll Be Home for Christmas**	8	20
50	O Holy Night**	12	24
38	Silver Bells*	9	21
42	Some Children See Him**	10	22
44	White Christmas**	11	23

Singers on the CD:
*Tanya Kruse, soprano; **Steven Stolen, tenor

Pianist on the CD:
Richard Walters

Violinist on the CD:
Christopher Ruck (tracks 4, 16)

Caroling, Caroling

Words by Wihla Hutson
Music by Alfred Burt

Do You Hear What I Hear

Words and Music by Noel Regney
and Gloria Shayne

where, Lis - ten to what I say! _____ The

Child; The Child, sleep - ing in the night; He will bring us good - ness and

light, He will bring us good - ness and

light. _____

The Christmas Song
(Chestnuts Roasting on an Open Fire)

Music and Lyric by Mel Torme
and Robert Wells
Arranged by Richard Walters

rein - deer _ real - ly know how to fly And so I'm of - fer - ing this

sim - ple phrase _____ to kids from one to __ nine - ty - two, al -

though _ it's been said __ man - y times man - y ways, Mer - ry Christ - mas,

Mer - ry Christ - mas to you. ____

Gesù Bambino
(with optional violin or cello obbligato)

Text by Frederick H. Martens
Music by Pietro A. Yon

* Omit small notes when performing this song with violin or cello.

an - gels sang, the shep-herds sang, The grate - ful earth re - joiced, _____ And at _ His bless - ed

birth the stars Their ex - ul - ta - tion voiced. _____ O come let us a -
opt: Ve - ni - te a - do -

Non troppo lento

dore Him, ___ O come let us a - dore Him, _____ O
re - mus, ___ Ve - ni - te a - do - re - mus, _____ Ve-

Violin
Gesù Bambino

Text by Frederick H. Martens
Music by Pietro A. Yon

This part may be carefully cut from the book.

continued on page 21

Cello
Gesù Bambino

Text by Frederick H. Martens
Music by Pietro A. Yon

This part may be carefully cut from the book.

continued on page 22

Violin

Cello

I Heard the Bells on Christmas Day

Music by Johnny Marks
Words by Henry Wadsworth Longfellow
Adapted by Johnny Marks
Arranged by Luke Duane

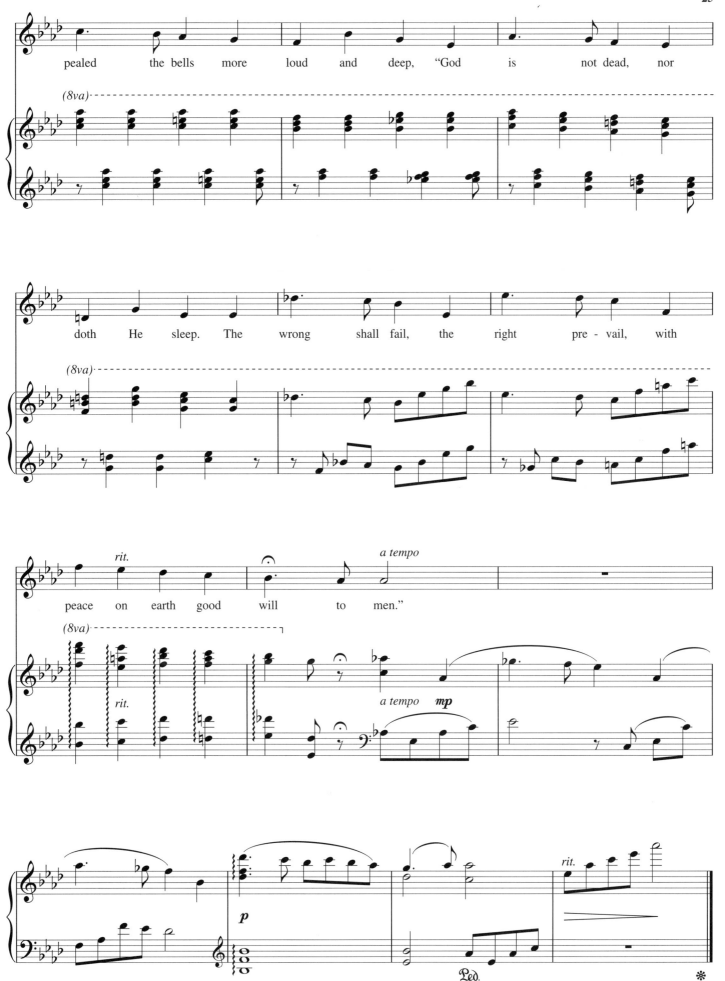

Go, Tell It on the Mountain

African-American Spiritual
Arranged by Harry T. Burleigh
Verses by John W. Work, Jr.

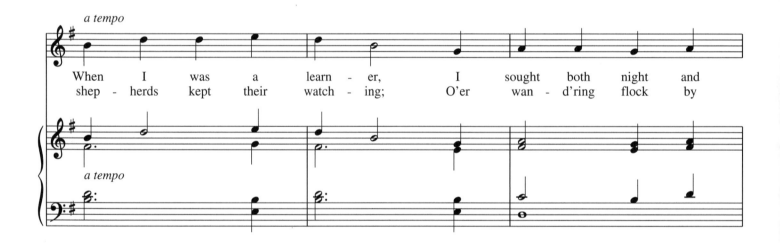

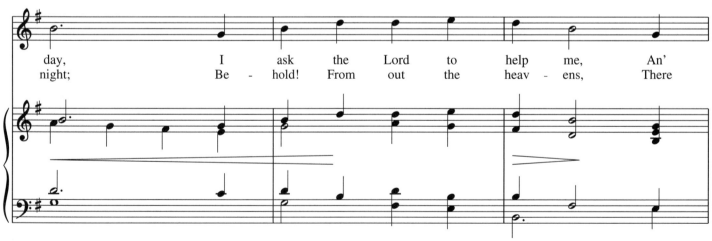

Burleigh's arrangement was originally titled "Go Tell It on De Mountains." The singular form "mountain" has become the standard version for this song.

He show me the way._____ Go tell it on the
shone a ho - ly light._____

moun - tain; O - ver the hills an' ev - 'ry - where:

Go tell it on the moun - tain, Our Je - sus Christ __ is

born.

On the companion recording we have eliminated this repeat (and the 3rd verse), because this setting may feel too long for some situations.

I Wonder as I Wander
(Appalachian Carol)

Collected, adapted, and arranged by John Jacob Niles

When Ma-ry birthed Je-sus, 'twas in a cow's stall, With

wise men and farm-ers and shep-herds and all. But high from God's heav-en a

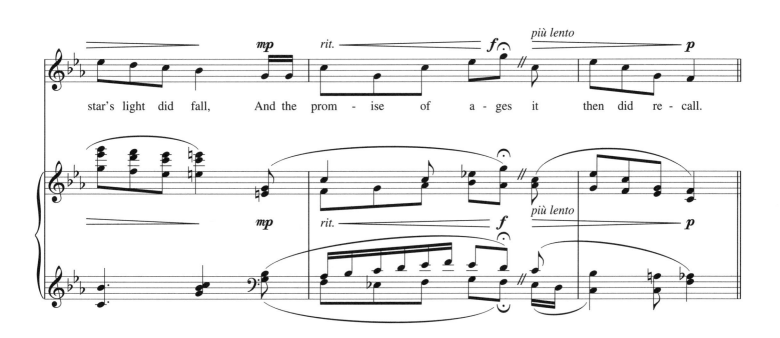

star's light did fall, And the prom-ise of a-ges it then did re-call.

I won-der as I wan-der, out un-der the sky, How

Je - sus the Sav - ior did come for to die For poor on - 'ry peo - ple like

you and like I... I won - der as I wan - der, out un - der the sky.

I'll Be Home for Christmas

Words and Music by Kim Gannon
and Walter Kent
Arranged by Luke Duane

Moderately slow

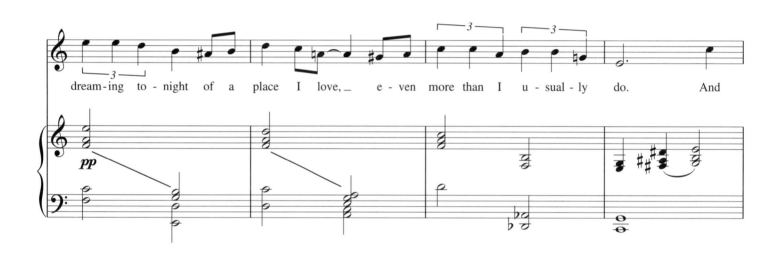

dream-ing to-night of a place I love, _ e-ven more than I u-sual-ly do. And

al-though I know it's a long road back, _ I prom-ise you

Silver Bells
from the Paramount Picture THE LEMON DROP KID

Words and Music by Jay Livingston
and Ray Evans
Arranged by Luke Duane

Some Children See Him

Lyric by Wihla Hutson
Music by Alfred Burt

tress - es soft and __ fair.
skin of yel - low __ hue.
filled with ho - ly __ light.
Some chil - dren see Him __ bronzed and brown, The
Some chil - dren see Him __ dark as they, Sweet
O lay a - side each __ earth - ly thing, And

Lord of heav'n to __ earth come down; Some chil - dren see Him bronzed and __ brown, With
Mar - y's Son to __ whom we pray; Some chil - dren see Him dark as __ they, And
with thy heart as __ of - fer - ing, Come wor - ship now the In - fant __ King, 'Tis

1,2
dark and heav - y __ hair.
ah! they love him __ too!

2. Some
3. The

3
love that's born to - night!

White Christmas
from the Motion Picture Irving Berlin's HOLIDAY INN

Words and Music by
Irving Berlin
Arranged by Richard Walters

and I am long-ing to be up north.

Espressivo

I'm dream-ing of a white

Christ - mas just like the ones I used to know

where the tree tops glis - ten and chil - dren

lis - ten to hear sleigh bells in the snow.

I'm dream - ing of a white

Christ - mas. With ev - 'ry Christ - mas card I write:

"May your days be mer - ry____ and bright,

and may all your Christ - mas - es be

white."

Where the tree tops glis - ten and

chil - dren lis - ten to hear

sleigh bells in the snow.

I'm dream - ing of a white Christ - mas;

with ev - 'ry Christ - mas card I write:

O Holy Night
(Cantique de Noël)

French Words by Placide Cappeau
English Words by John S. Dwight
Music by Adolphe Adam

vine! _____ O night,
ël! _____ voi - ci

O _____ night di -
le _____ Ré - demp-

vine.
teur.

dim.

mf

Tru - ly He taught us to love one an-
Le Ré - demp - teur a bri - sé toute en-

oth - er; His law is love and His Gos - pel is Peace.
tra - ve, La terre est li - bre et le ciel est ou - vert.

Chains shall He break, for the slave is our broth - er, And in His name all op - pres - sion shall cease. Sweet hymns of joy in grate - ful cho - rus raise we, Let all with - in us

Il voit un frè - re où né - tait qu'un es - cla - ve, L'a-mour u - nit ceux qu'en-chaî - nait le fer. Qui lui di - ra no - tre re - con - nais-san - ce? C'est pour nous tous qu'il

mf

cresc.

cresc.